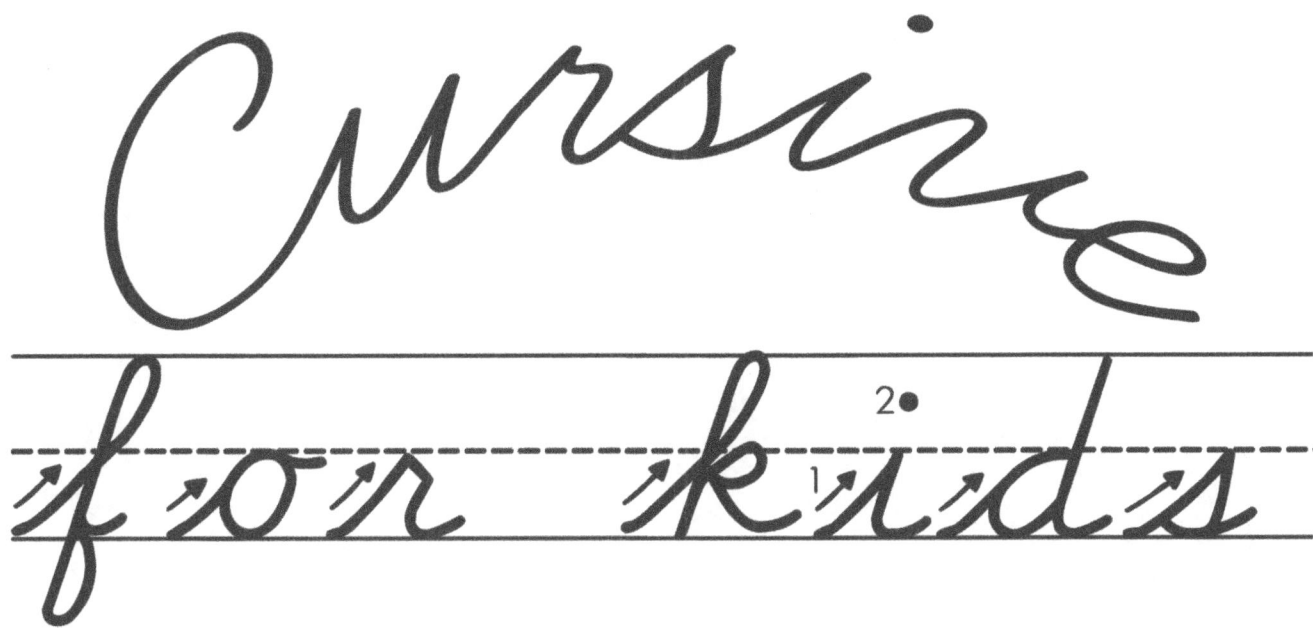

By: J. Steven Young

Cursive for Kids

(C) 2015 Tasicas-Young LLC

All Rights reserved. No part of this book may be reproduced or used in any way or form or by any means whether electronic or mechanical, this means that you cannot record or photocopy any material ideas or tips that are provided in this book.

Cursive for Kids

Holding your pen/pencil

Left handed   Right handed

Index "Pointing" finger

Thumb

Don't squeeze with index finger, Keep equal pressure from all fingers

J. Steven Young

J. Steven Young

Let's start by trying each letter - "BIG & small" - one time each!

Trace the letters

Aa Bb

Cc Dd

Ee Ff

Gg Hh

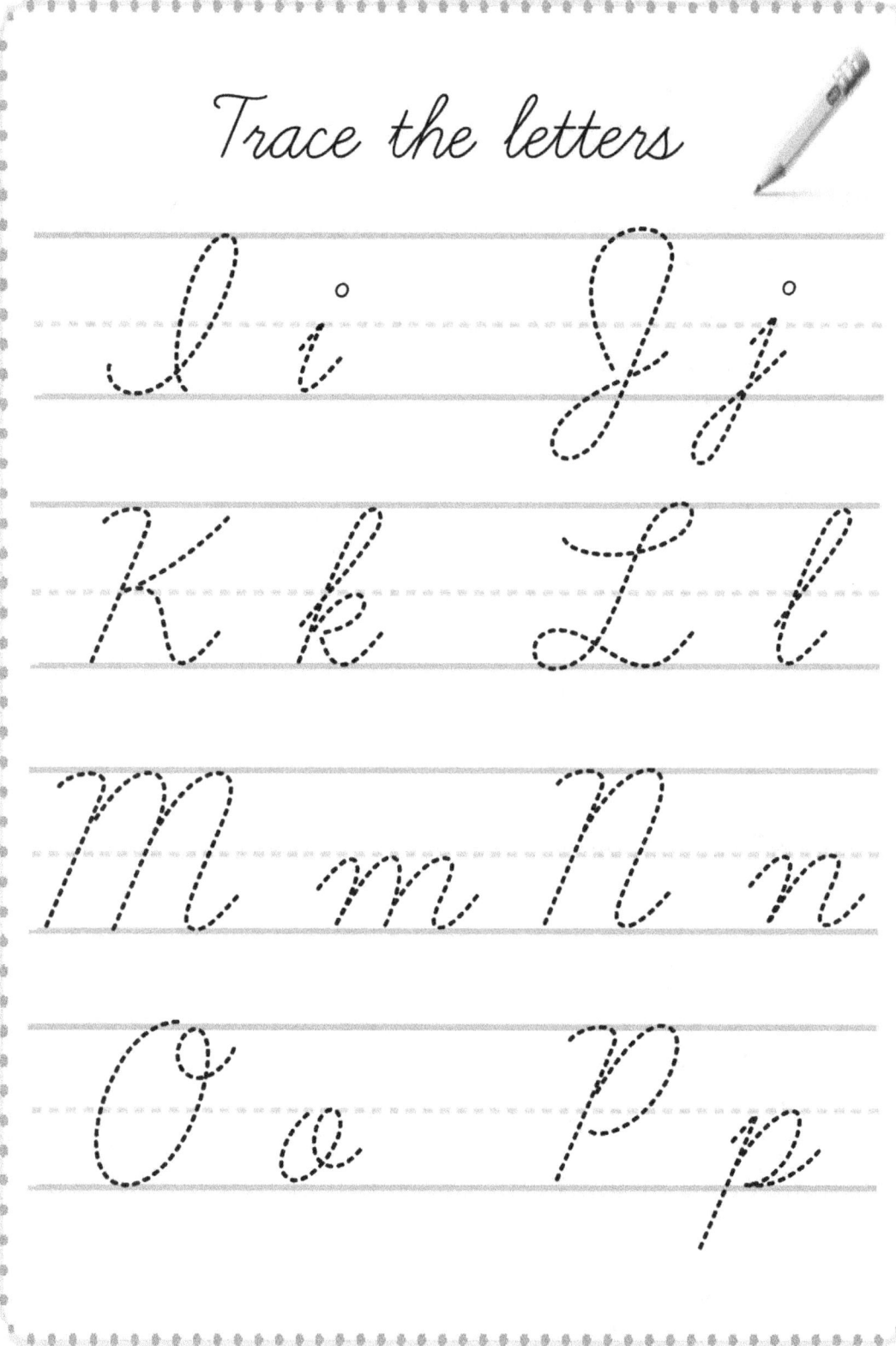

Trace the letters

Q q R r

S s T t

U u V v

W w X x

Trace the letters

Yy Zz

Writing letters... practicing multiple times with the same letter.

Sometimes there are many ways to write letters. See if you can tell the differences.

Follow the numbered steps for pen strokes on the following exercises.

Now try without help

𝒜 a

Now try without help

$\mathcal{B}$ b

Now try without help

C c

Now try without help

$\mathcal{D}\ d$

Now try without help

$\mathcal{E}$ e

Now try without help

$\mathcal{G}\ g$

Now try without help

Now try without help

l   i

Now try without help

K k

Now try without help

$\mathcal{L}$ l

Now try without help

M m

Now try without help

𝓃 𝓂

Now try without help

P p

Now try without help

2 q

Now try without help

$\mathcal{S} \quad s$

Now try without help

𝒰 𝓊

Now try without help

𝒰 𝓋

Now try without help

𝒲 𝓌

Now try without help

Now try without help

𝒴 𝓎

Now try without help

z z

Now try some words…

No tracing because you're getting GREAT at writing!

J. Steven Young

Try writing this word

cupcake

Try writing this word

eggplant

Try writing this word

giraffe

Try writing this word

house

Try writing this word

igloo

Try writing this word

monkey

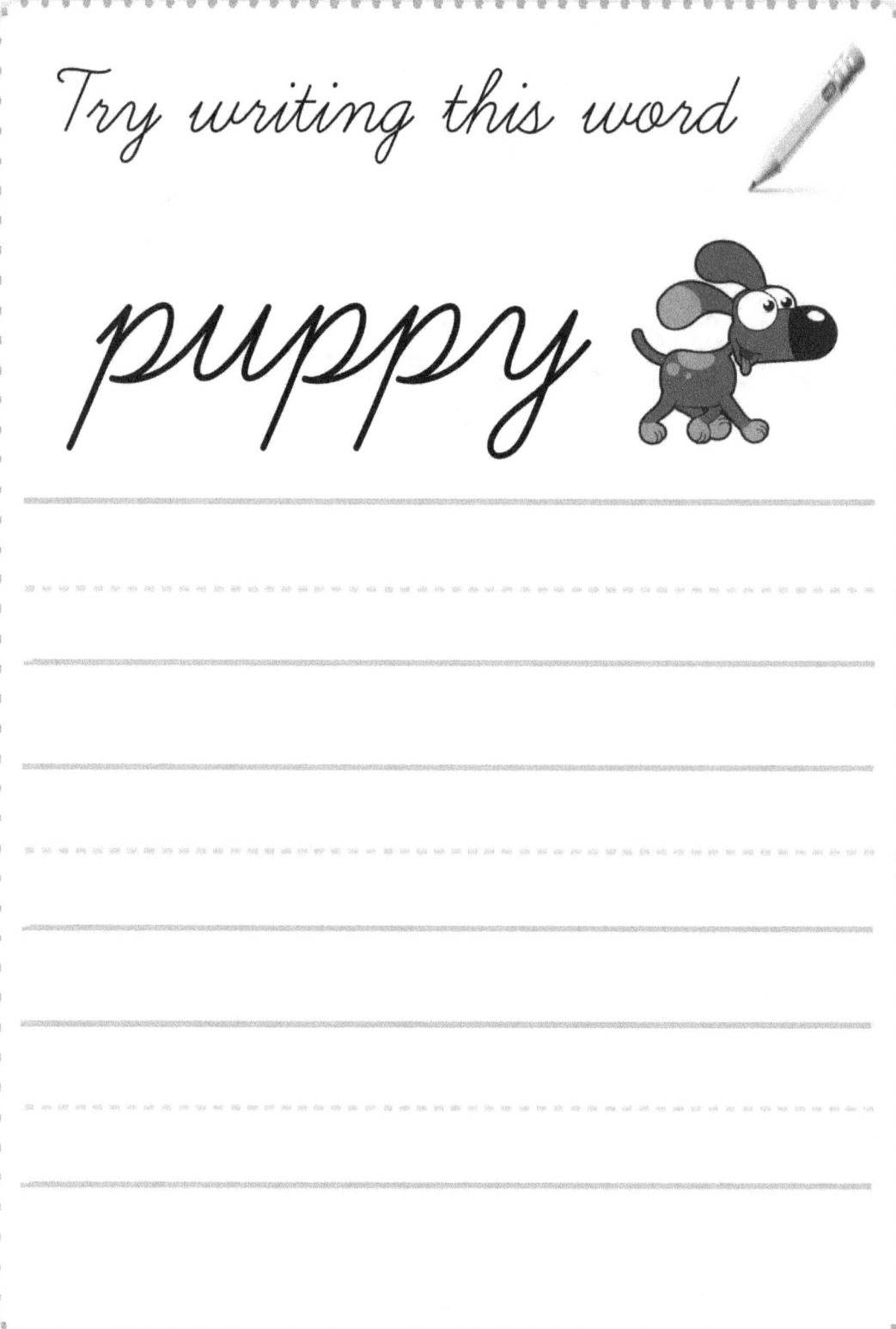

Try writing this word

queen

Try writing this word

rocket

Try writing this word

sun

Try writing this word

umbrella

Try writing this word

yo-yo

Try writing this word

zebra

Now try these common words

Aunt

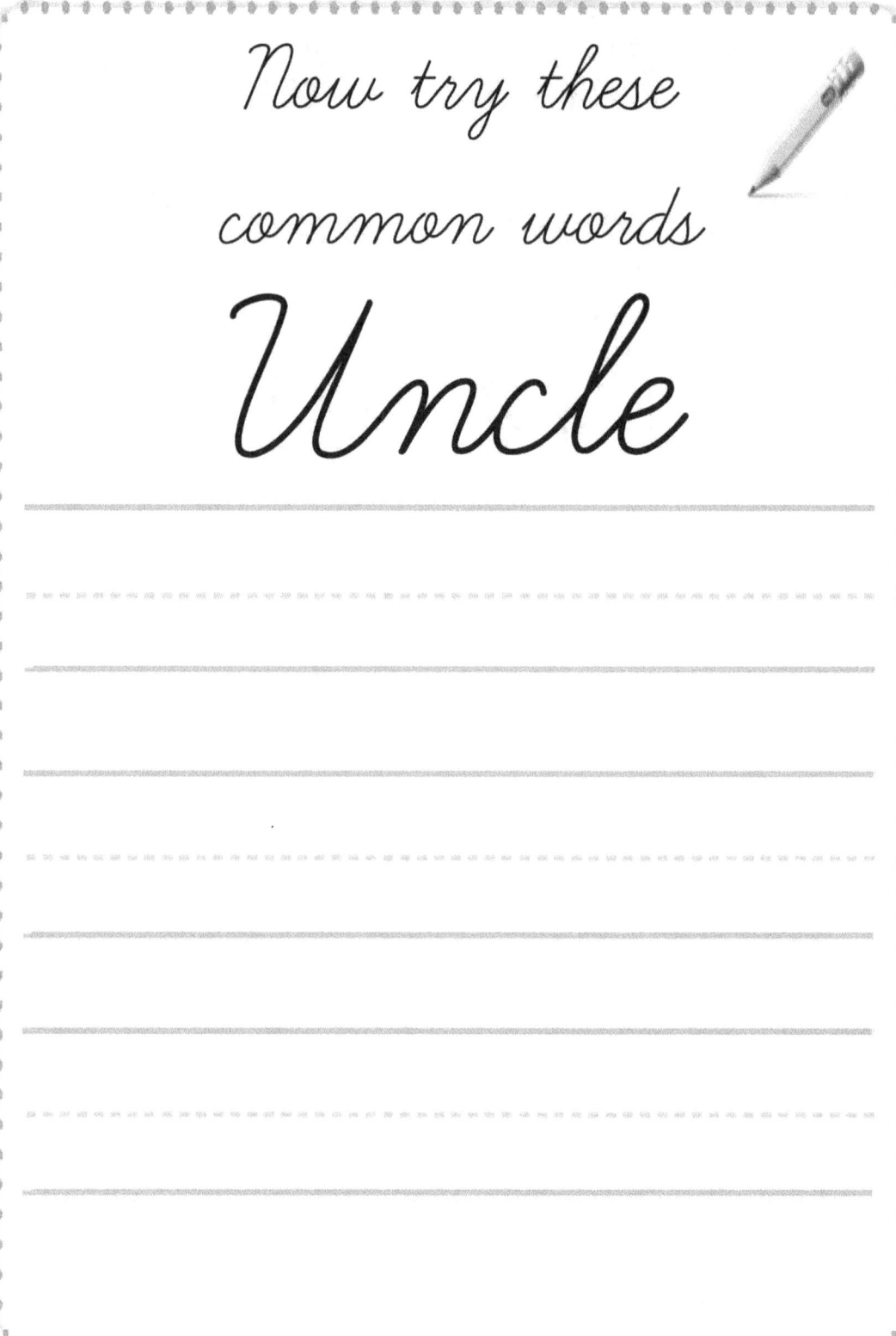

Now try these common words

Cat

Now try these common words

Dog

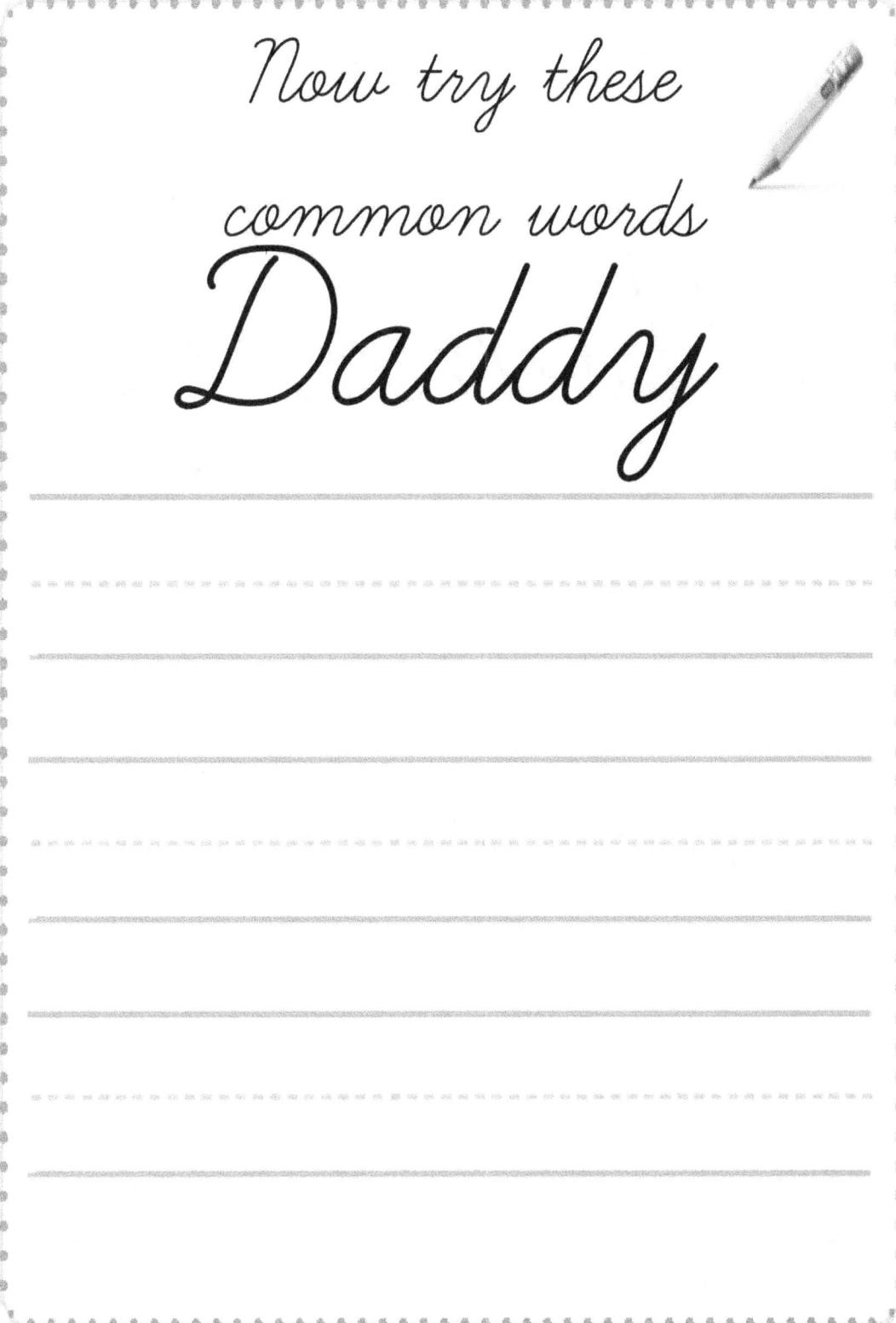

Now try these common words

Mommy

Now try these common words

Grandma

Now try these common words

Grandpa

Now try these common words

Fox

Now try these common words

Lazy

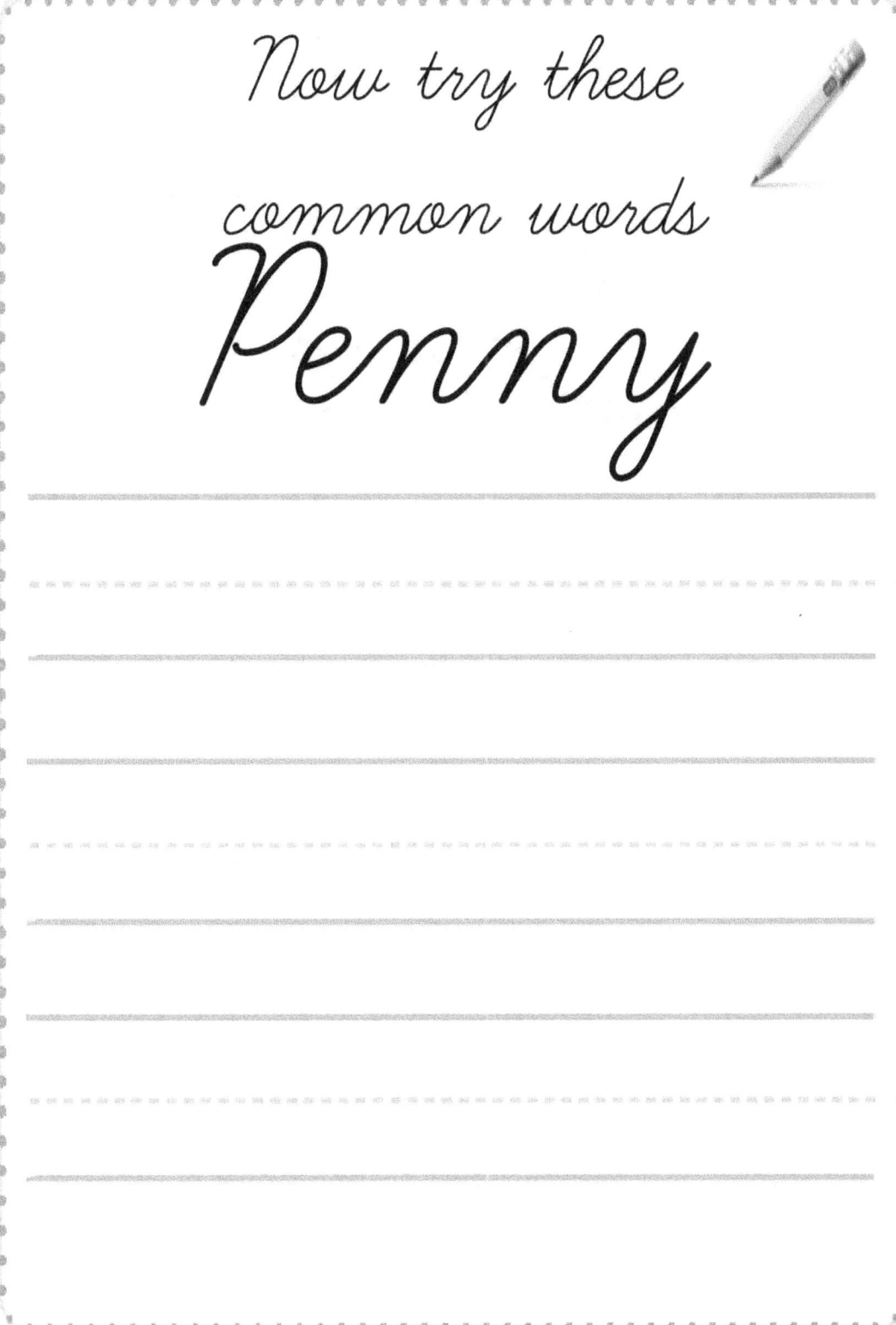

Now try these common words

Save

Now try these common words

Earn

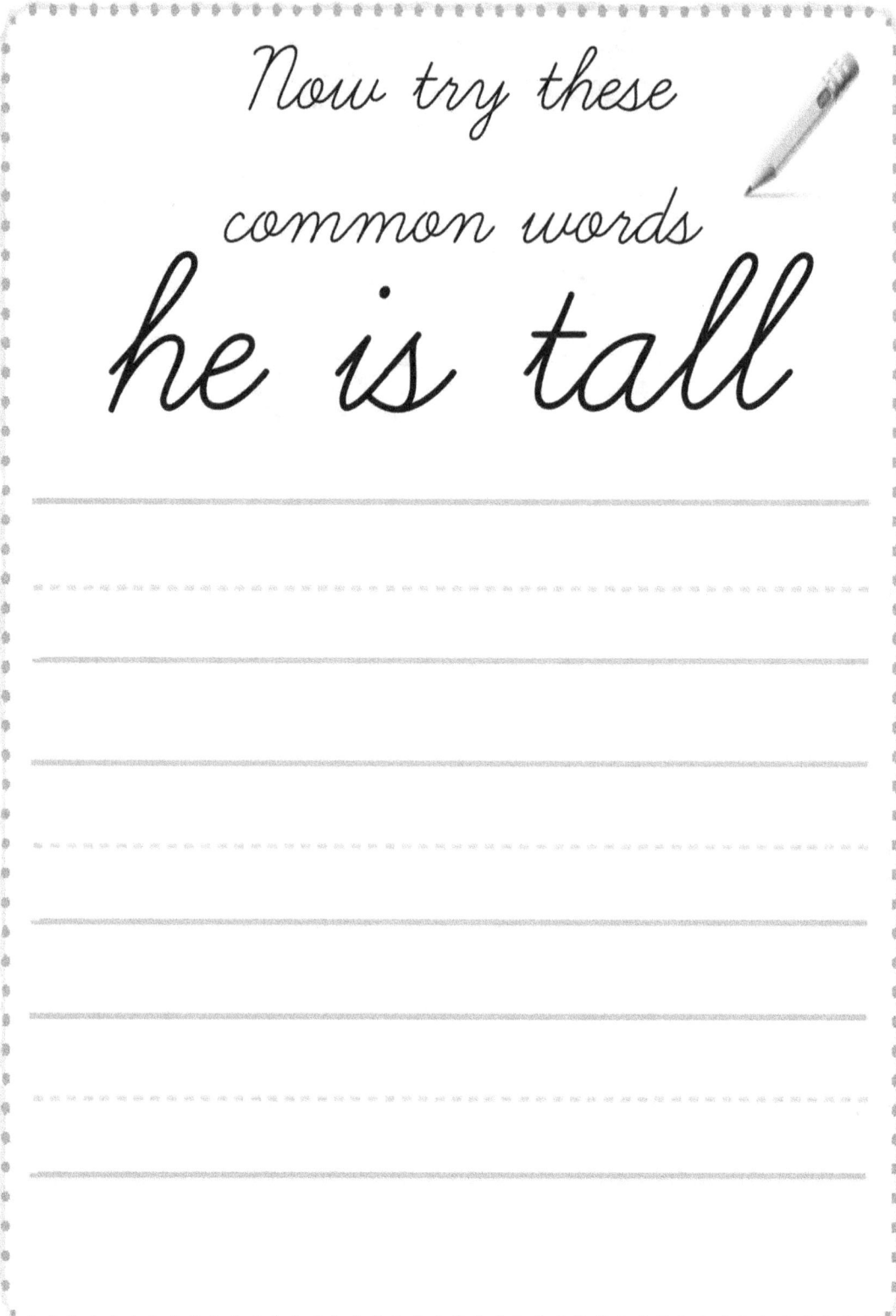

Now try these common words

truth

Now try these common words

over

Write this sentence...

"The quick brown fox jumped over the lazy dog."

Write this sentence...

"A penny saved is a penny earned."

Write this sentence...

"The truth is the strongest argument."

Practice writing your name.

Write a nice note to a friend

www.ingramcontent.com/pod-product-compliance
Lightning Source LLC
Chambersburg PA
CBHW081354080526

44588CB00016B/2492